FOR ALL THE WORLD TO SEE

And here
My beloved earth and cohabitants

we have the rare and luminous
Star Crested Liberationist

a fine and mellowed creature
of soul-sonic proportions.

Though known for their glamorous plumage
And flights of doubt-defying freedoms

The Star Crested Liberationist
more notably is a creature of remarkable autonomy

iridescently shining not for societal approval
but brilliantly by and for their own known emancipation.

Consequently
it is through such lavish self-appreciation

that the Star Crested Liberationist
is fabulously so adept

at lighting and divining such unshackling skies
for all the world to see.

MOUNTAIN SPELLS

poems by
Toussaint St. Negritude

Montpelier, VT

Mountain Spells ©2022 Toussaint St. Negritude
Release Date: October 22, 2024
All Rights Reserved.

Printed in the USA. First printing.

Published by Rootstock Publishing
an imprint of Ziggy Media LLC
Montpelier, Vermont 05602
info@rootstockpublishing.com
www.rootstockpublishing.com

Softcover ISBN: 978-1-57869-200-2
Library of Congress Number: 2024944038

Cover art "cosmographies in bloom" by Uncle Erok. Year made: 2023. Medium: Acrylic. Dimensions: 9x12" Artist's Instagram @uncle.erok and website: earthshinestudio.bigcartel.com. Used with permission.

Book design by Eddie Vincent, ENC Graphic Services.

The poem "Through The Wilderness" was published by the *Barre-Montpelier Times Argus*, on September 25, 2021.

The poem "Revelations In Lockdown" was published under the title "Revelations," in the locally self-published anthology of poems and photos, "Through The Window, Across The Road," 2020.

No part of this book may be reproduced or transmitted in any form or by any means whatsoever without express written permission from the publisher, except in the case of brief quotations embodied in critical articles and reviews. For reprint permission, email info@rootstockpublishing.com.

To schedule a reading, contact the author at stnegritude@gmail.com.

CONTENTS

FOR ALL THE WORLD TO SEE	iii
SHININGS OF THE DRUM	1
OUT IN MY YARD	3
COSMOGRAPHIES IN BLOOM	4
SINCE FOREVER	6
IN POTS BIG AS HUMAN DIGNITY	7
SOMETHING AIN'T ENOUGH FOR NOTHING	9
NEWS OVERHEARD FROM A LONG NIGHT'S JOURNEY	10
JUST ONE BOWL OF LOVE	11
WINGS JOYS TRUTHS & INNERMOST MEANS	12
LIKE ALICE IN THE GARDEN OF A SATCHIDANANDA DREAM	13
RISE AND SHINE	15
ELYSIAN TIME BUMP	16
PROPS TO THE PEOPLE	17
ALL GREEN LIGHTS	18
IF COLUMBUS STAYED HOME	20
REGARDLESS OF WHOM OR WHATSOEVER	22
SMALL TIME BOYS	24
MAROONING IN THE KEY OF NO BULSHITTING	26
PEEKABOO	28
THE LOVELIEST	29
THROUGH THE WILDERNESS	30
ALOFT WITHIN	33
WHY IS IT	34
THAT UNNATURAL QUESTION	35
THE OTHERING BLUES	36
THE IDIOCIES OF DENIAL	37
DEAD IN THE FACE	38
A WINTRY OBSERVANCE OF LOVE	40
JUST KEEP KEEPING	41
THIS SILENT SCRAMBLE	42
QUIT TAKING UP THE ROAD	43
FEELING FERN	44
WHY HATE LOVE?	45

ALL THIS GRACE	47
BROTHERS AND BROTHERS	48
HOW ABOUT NOW	50
BLUES OUT OF BOUNDS	51
CLIMBING HOME	52
I'M GONNA LET IT SHINE	53
ROCKING YOU	54
BLUES JEAN-MICHEL BASQUIAT	55
I'M GOING WITH HARRIET	56
BLUES FOR THE MASSES	58
ALL THESE DREAMS AND RIVERS AWAY	60
FOR THE YESES	63
REFLECTIONS OF A FUGITIVE HUMAN BEING	64
JUNE MOUNTAIN THUNDERSTORM	65
BLUESTERIA	66
THIS IS WHERE	67
SIDEWAYS BLUES	68
TO MAKE IT THROUGH	69
STRANGE CONES	70
STUNNING	71
RATTLING AT THE GATES	72
THE FREEING BLUES	74
CHEERS	75
SWIMMING THE AURORA	76
JAZZ KILIMANJARO	77
REVELATIONS IN LOCKDOWN	78
IT'S STAG SEASON	80
O HOLY THIS	82
HOW I BUILT MY STAR HOUSE	83
POET'S PROFILE	86

To the unmanned plan
of the mountains.

To their illuminating marronage
of our souls.

Hallowed be thy
gaze.

SHININGS OF THE DRUM

When the moon becomes the sun

I am the high-feathered reclaimer of Ouidah
via the port of Savannah and the waters of Bahia
of Cap Haitien and of Bayou St. Jean.

When the moon becomes the sun
I am the high-feathered scribe of Ghede
making mambo with our clothes off
shaking our graves and taking note.

When the moon becomes the sun

Well between the thighs of death and life
I am the listener and I am the voice.
I am the high-feathered seeds of jazz fleeing from our trials.

When the moon becomes the sun

Beyond the fog of our implied assimilation
I am the whispers of Dunbar Creek.
I am the high-feathered horns of the Black Star Liner.

When the moon becomes the sun

I am the drum of eminent reclamations.
I am the call of the unknown maroon.
I am the high-feathered calypso of a marching Black mob.

When the moon becomes the sun

I am the ascension of ancient melodies.
I am the chimes of hurricane blessings.
I am the listening of our dreams.

When the moon becomes the sun

I am the victory of 16 cowrie shells.
I am the Benin Palace of Madame Erzulie.
I am the shining of a well-seen voice.

When the moon becomes the sun

I am the votive envoy of La Place Guinee.
I am the call of the unknown maroon.
I am the high-feathered calypso of Ogun Batallah.

When the moon becomes the sun

I am the shining
I am the shining
I am the listening of Dunbar Creek.

OUT IN MY YARD

I love my stars.

Out where I live
I ain't got but 1 hundredth of an acre.

But I got 85,263 stars.
I got so many stars

Ain't no fence big enough
to keep 'em.

I love my stars.

Sometimes I'll walk a mile in the sky
just to see each and every one of them.

It I ain't got but a middle of a spittle
I'll be damned if I ain't got 85,263 stars

all shining brighter than a dime in
redemption.

I love my stars.
Ain't but a yard full of the universe.

I love my stars.
Just as pretty as a bowl full of bliss.

COSMOGRAPHIES IN BLOOM

Down a song flowing north
amid the boreal wilderness of innermost
transformation

appears the Realm
of the Soul-Rising Mountains
of the Moon at Dawn.

Obliged by the Gods
down a song of stars and coniferous
splendor

greens the calling
of reaches higher than our shadows
can modernly conceive.

Down a song flowing north
rises the Dawn-land of Illuminations:

welcoming the innermost of elevations
to passages of expansions
duly received.

Behold such noble means of galactic
introspection…

Behold each peak
surrounding each surrounding peak
upon peak upon peak.

Behold each bewitching reach…
Behold this ascension of Irrepressible Peace…

Behold your emancipation
from all dominions otherwise…
For here is where

your unconquerable wilderness
glistens in the liberty
your passion calls home:

welcoming all illuminations
to the Dawn-land incandescence of innermost
reclamations…

unshackling the sages from the ages
long now blazing and found.

Down this song flowing north
amid the boreal chicories
lining the cosmos from the astral floor

appears the Realm
of the Soul-Rising Mountains
of the Moon at Dawn.

Obliged by the Gods of Blossoming
Cosmographies…

Behold this land
your passion calls home.

SINCE FOREVER

Hallelujah goddamn

our future has been waiting
for so long now

our ancestors have been waiting
since forever.

Hurry up and get dressed
and put your good hat on.

Folks say tomorrow's
calling for sugar in all our bowls.

Hurry up now
and get on up those stairs.

Hallelujah goddamn

our future has been waiting
for so long

our moms
will be so pleased.

IN POTS BIG AS HUMAN DIGNITY

Once upon a time
there will be this thing called freedom.

Oh if I could only show you the view
from there:

Liberation for as far as your soul
can see.

We'll all be loving all the love
we please.

Once upon a time
there will be this thing called freedom.

By this point
folks will have consciously obliterated

all forms of bigotry
a long-long time ago.

No presumption of supremacy shall ever
be allowed there.

Once upon a time
there will be this thing called freedom.

We will know this to be true
because we have always known this to be true.

As is the artistry of the horn of the moon
the handiwork of our liberation

shall be painted clear across our lives
in all the spectral hues of translucent transformation

transcendentally raising all
ascendant affirmations.

Once upon a time
there will be this thing called freedom:

Liberation for as far as your soul
can see.

In pots big as human dignity
folks will be cooking up radicalizations of things

that today we couldn't even think
to believe.

There will be jazz and beats of people dancing
in the streets.

Folks will be so free
won't nobody remember any other way to be.

Oh if I could only show you the view
from there.

SOMETHING AIN'T ENOUGH FOR NOTHING

Back in the day
if you ain't had but 3/5ths of nothing

you might be able to turn
a tee-bit of nothing into something.

Nowadays
3 bits of something ain't enough for nothing.

You gotta be Charles Schwab
just to even turn the knob.

Ain't no room up in this inn
for me and all my kin.

Back in the day
we might find a patch of hay.

Nowadays
We out with the trash

be that
as it may.

NEWS OVERHEARD FROM A LONG NIGHT'S JOURNEY

Now
won't fit yesterday's shoes.

Today's
got a step only tomorrow can use.

We've got to
stretch into some broader views.

It ain't fit for nobody
to dream down a road of bad shoes.

JUST ONE BOWL OF LOVE

My mother

Having raised an entire
revolution

my mother
makes a whole loaf of freedom
from a bowl of access denied.

My mother

takes a spoonful of sugar
and a handful of courage
and sees to the horizons of boundless generations.

With the taste of sweet potato pie
and a generous amount of divine seasoning

my mother
has sweetened the courage of every step I take forward.

My mother
can nourish the consciousness of the entire table
from just one bowl of love.

My mother
Makes the whole world so much more livable

knowing full well
I love her more than a mere quarantine of miles
can ever tell.

I love my mother.

WINGS JOYS TRUTHS & INNERMOST MEANS

Live from your own heart of hearts
here's today's forecast:

Calling for gale-force harmonies.
Calling for showers of impromptu calming.
Calling for untold gusts of unauthorized
affirmations
with winds of free thinking epiphanies
reaching truth-scale speeds of up to a billion
renegade lifetimes per happiness.

Calling for elevations higher than age old fears.
Calling for all those with blues to breathe
to raise our wings
raise our joys truths and innermost means
and dig this gorgeous right
to simply resound
and gleam.

Calling for all unknown scales of peace
to blow in at such a pace

even you might just
feel the breeze.

And believe.

LIKE ALICE IN THE GARDEN OF A SATCHIDANANDA DREAM

Green as the day before
Columbus

like Perseids in perpetuity.

Green as hallelujahs in
bloom

the Orishas of our fruition
shall conjure beyond known bounds of comprehension

like melodies in receptivity

green as galaxies in
profusion

like orbs of Dolphy in connectivity.

Ours is a Dogon cosmology
in defiance of all colonization

leaping skies in seeds of wizardry.

We are that crystalline dignity
impervious to mono-scopic conclusions

shifting
the consciousness

like emissaries in perpetuity
like the Afrinicity of Obatala on a far northern street
like the frontiers of infinity

shifting
the consciousness

like Alice
in the garden of a Satchidananda dream

leaping whole categories
we are green as galaxies
in profusion

shifting
the consciousness

*like Alice
in a Satchidananda dream.*

RISE AND SHINE
(Or Seven Steps to Going Rogue)

Place your spirit above your head.

Gently step forward
leaving all boundaries behind you.

Leap mountainously towards your highest aspirations.

Land each foot squarely upon the high forest floor.
Position your emancipation as the basis of all steps further.

With your stars beaming thusly

rise and shine the vastness of your own pristine wilderness…
summoning your freedoms

to blossom as foretold.

ELYSIAN TIME BUMP

Ethnophonic
po-folks/bumping/
bomb-blasting repertoires
of b-flat and conjure/bumping/
snake-fingered tempos
into calisthenic wah-wahs/bumping/
emancipated jelly rolls
of clarinet and grandeur/bumping/
high and mighty high gris-gris
gone crazy/bumping/
casting neck-bone elations/bumping/
making elysian spells
out of old-born banjos
and whole note Haitians/bumping/
opening windows
onto haywire boogaloos/bumping/
clashing voices
with the stomping of some heavy storm/
bumping/
walking into birdland
in the key of Congo Square/bumping/
feeling mighty fine/bumping/
feeling mighty fine/bumping/
feeling mighty fine/bumping/
ethnophonic
po-folks/bumping/
walking Joplin
to the freedom sign/bumping.

PROPS TO THE PEOPLE

Jack be nimble.
Jack be hit by the fist of the U.S. Government.
Jack be trying to stagger
to his feet.
Jack be just another brother
trying to make ends meet.
Jack be beaten til the freedom bleeds.
Jack be the people marching
in the streets.
Jack be
what history calls
peace over my dead body.
Jack be nimble
as a riot.
Not come to hide
but to seek.
Jack be the dribble
to cause this whole ship to sink.
Jack be nimble
as a riot.
Not come to hide
but to seek.
Jack be the people marching
six feet deep.

ALL GREEN LIGHTS

i.

You can't stop a mountain
from standing on your toes.

You can't stop the sunrise
from Manhattan or Rome.

You can't stop the revolution
from ringing like bells.

And you can't stop me
from being myself.

ii.

You can't stop this message
from blooming in the hills.

You can't stop this harvest
from feeding who it will.

You can't stop this feeling
from going below the belt.

And you can't stop me
from being myself.

iii.

Not you.
Not your courts.
Not your rules.
Not your hatred.
Not your history.
Not your schemes.
Not your deception.
Not your collusion.
Not your lies.
Not your lies.
Not your lies.
Not your lies.
Not your lies.
Not your lies.

iv.

You can't stop this mountain
from seeing all your storms.

You can't stop this sunrise
from your gilding of thorns.

You can't stop this revolution
from ringing like bells.

And you can't stop me
From being myself.

IF COLUMBUS STAYED HOME

As the
world begins to boil
it becomes all the more clear
as if it hadn't been
abundantly apparent beforehand
what would have happened
if Columbus stayed
home
if the Mayflower
had veered towards the course of the Titanic
if all the arbiters
of the alleged New World
had stayed home
had stayed in Europe
if all their
mechanizations
and schemes of prosperity
had greedily ruined
all of their own
lands
had poisoned their own
waters
had spawned the diseases and ecological
catastrophes
and systemic generations of demoralizations
that could have better served
their own populations.

What would have happened
here on this land
and other lands of the globe
if Europe had simply
stayed home.
What billions of children
could have known the arms of their own cultures
their own languages
their own bodies
without the appointed loins
of modern civilization.

What would have happened
to this planet
if Columbus had simply stayed his ass
home

and the redwoods
just
kept growing.

REGARDLESS OF WHOM OR WHATSOEVER

I'm done with the system.

I don't want to work for it nor with it
nor towards its fabled salvage.

I'm done.

Please note my resignation effective
immediately.

The system has bound and slowed and
measurably penalized
every step I've known since birth

as can attest all births prior to my own.

All progressions achieved thus far and or
forwardly
are exclusively the fugitive results of life
beyond the grasp

of such ill-handed fuckery.
I'm done.

I'm done with the system.

And regardless of whom or whatsoever
sanctions
otherwise

without need
nor want of said regard

I'm done with the system.

Please note my resignation effective
immediately.

SMALL TIME BOYS

Small time boys
always sniffing at my joys

looking at my voice
licking at my toys.

Small time boys
dancing tantrums in my foils

pitching ransoms full of noise
thinking they can ride my passions with such teeny
little egos

full of such itty-bitty
swords.

Small time boys
falling fast around my poise

thinking God's hand almighty somehow graces
them
to storm my shores.

Small time boys
always sniffing at my joys

flipping colonies
in the guise of snake-skin lures.

Small time boys
better get from around my floors.

I'm a whole lot of reason
liberation gets to stomp the shit out of all them small time boys.

MAROONING IN THE KEY OF NO BULSHITTING

I'm a
Poet-Without-Permission
even a Jazz Musician.
A Healer-Without-Suppression.
I'm a
Dealer of Free-Ascensions.
I'm a
Poet-Without-Permission.
I don't heed
No prescribed notions of whitening authorizations.
I'm a
Dealer of Free-Ascensions.
I'm a
Poet-Without-Permission.
Free as our dreams
and all our fugitive constellations.
I'm a
Poet-Without-Permission
free as the maroons
of endless liberations.
I don't heed
no prescribed notions of whitening authorizations.
I'm a
Poet-Without-Permission
even a jazz musician.
I'm a Healer-Without-Suppression
flying wide
as a remedy full of emancipation.

I'm a
Poet-Without-Permission.
I'm a
Poet-Without-Permission.
I'm a
Poet-Without-Permission.

PEEKABOO

Just because
you close your eyes

doesn't mean
I'm not here.

Isn't that amazing?
It's remarkable

how profoundly I do
exist

with
or without your eyes.

THE LOVELIEST

On that occasional
cool 45° New England August evening

after a lingering afternoon
in the high hot 80s°

I often love to
drape a backwoods stroll

with a nice wrap of mink
and high-laced boots

adding just enough extravagance
to a sparkling star-lit pair of cut-off shorts.

Occasionally
I too am the loveliest man

The moon
Has ever seen.

THROUGH THE WILDERNESS

Through the wilderness
of my freedom

through territories
uncharted for corporate
consumption

through cogent dreams
and cosmic streams

I have climbed
to find my Star House
high amongst the peaks

of an ever-emancipating
consciousness.

Through these constellations
strewn within my
soul

here I have climbed
to find my sanctuary

housing
all the juju this new day
can hold.

Through days clouded
in the valleys of self-deceit

through the darkest
immobility of shacking
bigotries

through hours journeyed by prayer and by hand
and by feet

through hell
and high-water indignities
dangling inequities
for the hungriest to eat

through powers stronger
than all the calls
for my defeat

I have climbed
to find my Star House

high amongst the peaks
of my own true
belief.

Through declarations
flowing from the sovereignty of peace

through the clear and present
affirmation

that the Universe
is inalienably mine
to reach

through this connectivity
of all my soul to keep

through the envisioning
of a sanctuary deep within my
truth

I have climbed
to find my Star House

high amongst the peaks
of a bright and fertile liberty
built for innermost use.

ALOFT WITHIN

Like any divine worship:
my love of the mountains is humbled from their
feet.

You can't climb God.
You can try.

But you can't see Everest
from the top.

WHY IS IT

Why is it that
when I

stand up and say:
why not black?

The room returns an echo
suggesting I put my words back.

And back & back & back
I sit

all goodied and
clean.

"Who… Toussaint?" they say.
Oh he don't

Oh he don't
Oh he don't mean a thing.

THAT UNNATURAL QUESTION

By definition
of the very word itself

how can any aspect of nature
ever be unnatural

irregular or worse yet
unbecoming

for me and my natural self
to be?

THE OTHERING BLUES

In the human context:

to be mis-specied
is to be identified as being of

some perceived species
which is thought to be less than

what is known as
the human species.

In any given
any given

any given interaction with what I know to be
humanity:

I am mis-specied
every time I step within view.

Perhaps this happens
to you too

when humanity
fails to see its own hue.

THE IDIOCIES OF DENIAL

How many massacres?
How many acts of racism?

How many assaults on our humanity?
How many repetitions of genocide?

How many mechanizations of systemic greed?
How many destructions of our collective ability to survive?

How many drying sources of water?
How many dwindling sources of sanity?

How many collective idiocies of denial?
How many collective idiocies of denial?

How many collective idiocies of denial
does it take to screw in a light bulb?

How much time
You got?

Yeah no matter
How many times it happens

We never seem to see
The light.

We never seem to see
The light.

We never seem to see
The light.

We never seem to see
The light.

DEAD IN THE FACE

There are
several ways to handle a fight.

For some folks
it's an eye for an eye.
If someone hits you 3 times
you hit them three times.
If someone hits you 23 times
you hit them 23 times.
If someone hits you
dead in the face
you make sure you hit them dead in the face 10
times harder.

For some folks
who have been hit 100s of times for hundreds of
years
and have never hit back
never called for justifications of war
never returned one pounding punch of all the
throws
that still continue to malign the faces of a future
that only looms for more

for some folks
who might be ready to bring all vengeance to the
judge's door

there are
several ways to handle a fight.

How this ends
won't be just another treatise of promised
rice.

A WINTRY OBSERVANCE OF LOVE
Honoring Martin Luther King Jr. Day

Slain heroes
don't quite whisper
like cedar trees in the far northern breeze.

Slain heroes
don't quite anesthetize
these icy inequities still dangling from our
dreams.

Slain heroes
never quite warm
to the cooperative shiverings of complicity.

Slain heroes
howl
loud and feared.

Slain heroes
of love
don't quite ever ever disappear.

JUST KEEP KEEPING

I love how
progress makes its own path

how the act of simply going forward
makes its own path

how the clearest paths we know
are simply the results

of a whole lot of going
forward.

I love hoe
despite the coldest unknowns

how a
whole lot of movement of our own movements

just keep keeping us
going forward.

THIS SILENT SCRAMBLE

Meeting
your white friends parents
is always a cultural endeavor

especially
when your white friends insist on being
even more clueless than their parents.

It becomes such a silent scramble
to then pirouette
between flying daggers

and trenching
rounds of automatic denials.
While I

Blackening-for-my-life
am guessing who's not coming for dinner
never to be seen again.

QUIT TAKING UP THE ROAD

White privilege
straddles down the road

not along the shoulder
but straddles all across the street

all across
the middle of what should be decency

just so
(just in case the world didn't fully understand)

just so
all the world could plainly see

just for whom
all roads do supremely meet.

FEELING FERN

Honoring my dear friend Fern Feather (1992-2022), and all who are assailed by hate

I love his light
and his walking truth.

I love the feel
of her gleaming sorority.

I love their feeling the courage
to simply be and to bloom.

And for however many times
Fern was stabbed

I ache and bleed from every wound.
So many of us do.

Only fern's smile
blooms me through and through.

WHY HATE LOVE?

Look
fuck all you idiots
who just can't grasp the fact that who I love
how I love
and how good that love is
ain't got shit
to do with
you.

The world spins forward
whether you dig it or not.

A globe set in motion
is not for backward glances.

I am
and will be loved irrepressibly
and in conjunction
and in return
I shall love most naturally
fantastically
in the light
and in the streets.

My love is a declaration nothing can defeat.

This is a love
like all good loves.
Dig love and love shall dig you free.

No need to hate the music.
just go on and love your own sweetness
while I go on and sweetly love the love I love
liberally
constitutionally

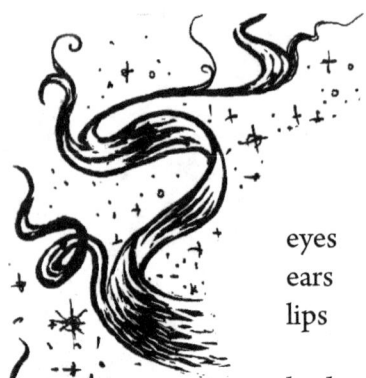

eyes
ears
lips

body mind and
soul.

Besides
regardless of the fools who beg to differ
this love
doesn't give a shit who dares to quibble.

This love will kick the ass of denial
Every which way the heart blows.

This love is beautiful.

This love
makes the Louvre lose its speech.
This love
walks on water and keeps the beat.
This love
can shine through walls 50-states thick.

You can't fuck with this.

So why hate love?

You better
recognize this sweetness.

ALL THIS GRACE

I'm so sorry
I know you'd love to hate me

But much to your chagrin
my humanity is just much too much

for even you to withstand.
I know

you'd love to detest my face
but much

to your own wretchedly vile disgrace
my badass beauty

just keeps shining with every last look you take.
I know I know

how could God create all this grace?
Step aside little world

I'm about to light this goodness from here
to outer space.

Gold don't spoil for nobody.
No matter what they say.

BROTHERS AND BROTHERS

Brothers and brothers.
Brothers and brothers in arms of other brothers.

Brothers and brothers.
Brothers and brothers loving brothers in arms of
other brothers loving brothers.

Brothers and brothers.
Brothers and brothers in arms being brothers

being lovers
being brothers being mothers

brothers being sisters
brothers being rescuers

brothers and brothers being keepers of brothers
in love
with other brothers.

Brothers and brothers in arms of other brothers.
Brothers and brothers.

Brothers and brothers loving brothers.
Brothers of breath and thunder

holding the one love that can not be shut
asunder.

Brothers and brothers holding the one love
that can not be shut asunder.

Brothers of breath
and thunder.

Brothers and brothers breathing life!
Brothers and brothers breathing life!

Brothers and brothers loving brothers in arms of other brothers
loving brothers

breathing life!
breathing life! *(...deep inhale, and release)*

HOW ABOUT NOW

When nobody's looking
do Black lives still matter?

How about now?
How about when my mother

goes to the doctor?
How about when I cross the street?

Do I get to use the crosswalk too?
How about when the chickens come home to roost?

How about when I've told you to get your hands off me?
How about

when nobody's looking?
Do Black lives still matter then?

Even if everybody's still telling
the truth?

How about now?

BLUES OUT OF BOUNDS

Out of hand
out of mind
out of the way
outside
out of town
out of reason
out of history
out of mysteries
out of listening
out of time
out of signs
out of rhyme
out of dreams
out of means
out of size
out of freedom
out of keys
out of eyes
out of climbs
out of skies
out of skies
out of skies
we are deemed but to rise
out of freedoms dreamed out of lives greened
out of bounds.

CLIMBING HOME

I have been climbing can't-do's all my life.

I have scaled every doubt
this great land of the free has assailed my way

and I'm still here

scaling every cant-do this old world
has to offer.

Ain't a can't-do high nor lawful enough
to keep me from climbing

to where or what or who I need to be.

I have been climbing can't-do's all my life
and I'm still here

scaling my way to yonder-be.

I'M GONNA LET IT SHINE

Not knowing what is to come

I stand on the banks of tomorrow
and my soul looks vast and wonders

how in the world
any other vision could ever be so fine.

I stand on the banks of tomorrow
and my soul looks vast and wonders

to which flowing glory
shall I rise divine.

I stand on the banks of tomorrow
and my soul looks vast and wonders

my feet may be bound
by the shores of a current denial

but with this little light of mine
I can fly like a bird in the sky

I can fly like a bird in the sky.
Not knowing what is to come

I stand on the banks of tomorrow

wondering how in the world
any other vision could ever be so fine.

ROCKING YOU

Dear 25 year old me,
I'm sorry to say I've stepped into the future

some 35 years from now
only to discover that dreams of precious boyfriends

fade just as ghostly
as affordable housing.

And it turns out that America

really has no interest
in rocking you

like a hurricane
but actually prefers the presumed calm of fascism.

And apparently
what turns out to be far worse than the
presumption of liberty

is the absolute absurdity
of believing we had ever belonged.

Please do believe in me.
And please do disturb the peace.

BLUES JEAN-MICHEL BASQUIAT

I know why
the caged bird bit the hand
he was dealt
and flew the fuck away.

I know why
the caged bird said fuck this shit
and chewed
that lock to bits.

I know why
The caged bird does not dream
Of his captor's
yield.

Bird flying high.

I know how you
Feel.

I'M GOING WITH HARRIET

I don't know
how many of you are with me on this

or how you might want to do as you wish.
But I would be totally remiss
if I didn't say in all seriousness

I am not going back.

Y'all can yearn and pine
for status quo's return all you want.

But I ain't going back.

Send my regards to capitalist greed
the same irrational creed that has now left you
to writhe and bleed.

But I am not going back.

I am not going back
to that plantation that has dogged me to my
knees.

I am not going back
to the treachery that has denied my most vital
need to fabulously simply be me.

I'm not going back
to your complicit country 'tis of thee.

The buck stops here.
Y'all can return to death as you wish.

I will stake my fortunes
on the livelihood of mountains far from all this.

The currency of my survival
is as free as the stars from which I exist.

The fruition of this garden
blossoms to a higher time and bliss.

Y'all can wait
for what thrills your master's lash.

But I ain't going back
for none of this.

BLUES FOR THE MASSES

Honoring Reuben Jackson

Remember when our intelligence
was a thing?

Remember that?
Remember when Human Intelligence

was the ticket to moving forward
when wisdom won the race

when that which separates
a bad road from a good road

was one's ability to align the stars
and go?

Remember when Human Intelligence
discovered things

built things
solved things

answered things
wrote things

sang things
moved things

summoned things
believed things

loved things
that otherwise seemed impossible?

Remember when Human Intelligence
was a thing?

When the smartest way forward
was your own?

ALL THESE DREAMS AND RIVERS AWAY

{meditations i.}

Waking up free!
Me and the ancient me who first broke free of
slavery in 1619.
Me who followed the Powhattan River to the
Appalachian peaks.

Me and the future me who just broke free of slavery
in the year 2019.
Me who followed the path of my own liberty.
Waking up free!

Me east of where Dowabodiwadjo speaks.
Waking up free by the waters of Lake Willoughby.
Me astrospectively

Seeing freedoms where freedoms ought to be.
Infinitely waking up free.
Waking up free!

Waking up free
all these dreams and rivers away
from 400 years of slavery.

Me and the present me who will always be free of
boundary
all these dreams and rivers away
from 400 years of slavery.

{meditations ii.}

Waking up free
in the brook-green-forest-opening of my own truth-green-focused
wilderness:

spruce-top evidence
of an ebullient consciousness
here for the luminescence.

Here in the fugitive mountainry
of letting go of everything but the blessings
of a high-ridge transcendence.
Feeling
the inner-passage
of an astral vastness.

Waking up free
far beyond the madness
far beyond the sovereignty of ashes and the democracy of deceit.

Waking up free
from the chattel bondage of compliance
and somebody else's greed.

Waking up free
self-freed and released
from the mordant hounds of those so determined

to cease all peace.
I'm here for the belief
in the illuminating liberties of all the stars we seek

feeling beyond the periphery
into worlds not even the most titled of eyes
can see.

Waking up free
all these dreams and rivers away
from slavery.

Taking the leap / feeling the means.
Waking up free to be seen by me: free as jazz
and the air I breathe.

FOR THE YESES

Effervescent
lessons
of pleasures
treasured
essence

measured
blessings
of incandescent
vexes

pulsing
guesses
transcendent
ledges
of joy meets joy
dancing
upon
the
nexus

glancing
upon
the majestic
of a wilderness
green
for
the
yeses

heart-wise
hexes
dancing
upon
the
nexus.

REFLECTIONS OF A FUGITIVE HUMAN BEING

Water-freed breeze
and you and few and far between

great blue herons approve this life
bemused of stars and dreams

skinny-dipped
in powers of dawn and trees.

Moons arise
from journeys home

and long believed loons confide
in howls of glee.

Nothing defies one's liberty
bound by the powers of the water-freed breeze.

JUNE MOUNTAIN THUNDERSTORM

Water
rolling orders
water
flashing courses
water
shuffling boulders
water
seeding forces
water
tolling shoulders
water
lightning orders
water
rolling borders into portals into portals into portals
water
rolling shoulders
within the corners of the universe
water
casting orders into bloom
water
casting orders into bloom
water
casting orders into bloom.

BLUESTERIA

In the emerald spell
Of the morning snowlight shading east

hazing daylong dusk
beyond this cold clock's relief

there's the most enshrining
air of bluesteria

that frailing condition of flatted
gris-gris

a queer intuition of fog
and witness

divining the silence
to flash… and speak.

In the diaphanous will
Of my own gracing peace

there is the most beguiling
recognition of bluesteria

sounding my wildest interiors
to sing and reap

divining my horizons
to expand and receive.

THIS IS WHERE

I like
climbing deep
into the forests of my soul

and deciding
right then and whole:
this is where I shall build my home

and flourish
as a mountain black and old.

SIDEWAYS BLUES

Snow blowing in
sideways strong.

Snow blowing in
all sideways long.

And if this snow don't mind
my sideways bones

I'll be leaning in
to feel its sideways song.

I'll be leaning in
all sideways long.

Snow blowing in
sideways strong.

TO MAKE IT THROUGH

Hauling wood
hauling water
hauling all the hope I can afford

to make it through
make it true
make it up the hill til Kingdom's blue.

Hauling all the hope
to make this old world
worth its coat and use.

Hauling dreams
the size of my very own boots.

Hauling wood
til the whole mountain
shakes this winter loose.

Hauling wood
hauling roofs.

STRANGE CONES

I love this time in Vermont

when the gunfire
sounds like Philadelphia
or Oakland or Chicago
or wherever the police steadily serve and protect.
Pop pop pop pop POP!
Pop pop pop pop POP!

I love this time in Vermont

when Bernie
and Trump voters alike
can join arms in full triggering fervor.
Pop pop pop pop POP!
Pop pop pop pop POP!

The way the telltale red
starts to bleed across the maples
amid the strange
cones of northern fragility

as the white-hooded warblers
prepare their rightful
journey south.

I love this time in Vermont.
Pop pop pop pop POP!
Pop pop pop pop POP!

Such a lovely autumnal affair.

STUNNING

Smiling skies
of simmering spells

swimming of beards abloom
and sunny.

Today's forecast
is fabulously stunning

in swells attuned
of peanut butter and honey.

Fabulously stunning

swimming of beards abloom
and sunny.

RATTLING AT THE GATES

Always
a fool for fire

my heart's
been burned more times
than a broom
in a room full of lightning.

And here I am

bodily storming
cosmically torching
fluttering my longing
throbbing
and informing
my swollen love of a man
whose eyes are
sorcerously adorable

whose smile
sends me vascularly soaring.

So elegant is his beard

that in its wilderness
I plan on being lost for years on years.

And here I am

bodily storming
candidly roaring
flaming across borders
shaming doctor's orders

rattling at the gates
of would-be glories
could be portals

stories of a boy
who says I love you
I see you
I feel you:

cosmically scorching
bodily storming

all for the love
of a man whose eyes
are so fantastically
adorable.

THE FREEING BLUES

No need in lying
I ain't trying
to be nobody's fool

but what you got
has got me
flying with no shoes.

I've lost all rules
and dropped outta
school.

You got me
freeing
the blues.

And I ain't about
to let this good thing
loose.

CHEERS

Some people you like
until you fuck

and then you're like
"what was I thinking?"

Some people you like
until the beer wears off

and then you're like
"good grief."

You
I've always really liked.

You're still good
No matter what I'm thinking.

I can drink you
All day long.

SWIMMING THE AURORA

Falling
In love with you

releasing what's held behind
and plunging

going below the surface
into the ether

and re-emerging
like Arcturus

firing above the consensus
into the ether

with you.

JAZZ KILIMANJARO

As a Jay-bird
naked
as so help me God
naked
as a heart seen out loud
naked
as a feeling full of cause
naked
as the freeing at all odds
naked
as this here mountain found high above the clouds
naked
as this calling deep within our song.

As a Jay-bird
I am naked as the Kilimanjaro Flower.

Enough already
with the cloaking hour.

Show me what sings.
Show me what rings.
Show me what beams your sun to shower
and shower
and shower
and shower.

REVELATIONS IN LOCKDOWN

If ever
there was a day
a week
several months
if there was ever a place in time
where all
you could ever be
is yourself
would that ever be enough?

If all you could ever be
is yourself

would that ever be enough?
If you couldn't be
the worker
the desk worker
the customer service worker
the beloved worker
the dutiful worker
the tired worker
the abused worker
the approved worker
the awarded worker
the well paid worker
the liked worker
the unseen worker
the uncared for worker
the neglected worker

the local worker
the required worker
the unpaid worker
the broken worker
the poorly paid worker
the demanded worker
if you couldn't be anything beyond your own
front door

if for maybe forever
if you couldn't ever be anything but yourself

would that ever
be enough?

IT'S STAG SEASON

It's Stag Season

which is no euphemism
for sexy singles.

Stag (short for Stagnation Season)
is that swarmiest time during the summer

when impending rain storms
loom

at their heaviest threat
promising an Amazonian deluge fit for
atmospheric change.

Yet until such expecting occurrence
Stag Season can hang

in mid air
for days into weeks

leveraging a stillness
of abject humidity

an abominable hesitancy
rendering an eternity

of sweat-maddening hours
of no seen relief

no noon or evening sleep.
It's just Stag Season

til the good cloud
deigns to weep.

O HOLY THIS

Late swim
On a groovy twilight bliss.

I am but a supplicant
Of this heart-wise kiss.

Heaven is but a dew-drop
of this skinny-dipped bliss.

I am but a supplicant
Of this heart-wise kiss.

HOW I BUILT MY STAR HOUSE

It started
with making poems

seeing the alchemic results
of pairing transcendence

with
the trodden floor

taking the seeds of some-way-forward
and adding palpable visions from a river

of things
yet to be seen

building modes of liberation
from roads of inner-born means.

Then it began to flourish
through the making of hats

through the creation of crowns
anointing each vision I grasped

turning poems
into high-feathered hats.

And with colors of courage
and destinies blessed

with the galactic clarity
of an incandescent breath

whole poems began to sound
from the far outer reaches

of a blown
bass clarinet.

Soon entire cosmographies of freedom
began to speak into being

reap into healing
reach into seeing

freeing into believing
feeling into gleaning my way home.

It started
with making poems

turning mountains
into navigational tomes

finding marronage
upon these high-ridge bones of futures

crowning
to be shown.

It started
with making vessels

from dreams
forest grown.

It started
with making the asterism

of a
drinking gourd

into the castle
of my very own home.

And thus…
is born the Star House.

It started
with making poems.

POET'S PROFILE

Former Poet Laureate of Belfast, Maine, and 2024 nominee for the Poet Laureateship of Vermont, poet, bass clarinetist, and composer Toussaint St. Negritude conjures whole liberations in full tempo. The late US Poet Laureate (1985-86) Gwendolyn Brooks once described his work as "full of sweet sounds and surprises." His poetry has been published in *Michigan Quarterly Review, Birchsong, Philadelphia Stories, Savannah Literary Journal, PoemCity*, and the *San Francisco Bay Guardian*.

Originally from San Francisco, Toussaint has lived and broadly thrived across the African Diaspora, from the sacred mountains of Haiti, to the Coltrane District of North Philadelphia. He, along with bassist Gahlord Dewald, is the leader of the band Jaguar Stereo!, a free-form ensemble of his own poetry and improvisational jazz. His works have been widely published and recorded for over 40 years. On an alpine sanctuary facing east, Toussaint St. Negritude continues to thrive in the farthest elevations of Vermont's Northeast Kingdom. *Mountain Spells* is his first traditionally published volume of poetry.

We Grow Our Books in Montpelier, Vermont

Learn more about our titles in Fiction, Nonfiction, Poetry and Children's Literature at the QR code below or visit www.rootstockpublishing.com.

www.ingramcontent.com/pod-product-compliance
Lightning Source LLC
Chambersburg PA
CBHW070241090526
44586CB00035B/1374